Wake up, Father Bear

Story by Beverley Randell
Illustrations by Isabel Lowe

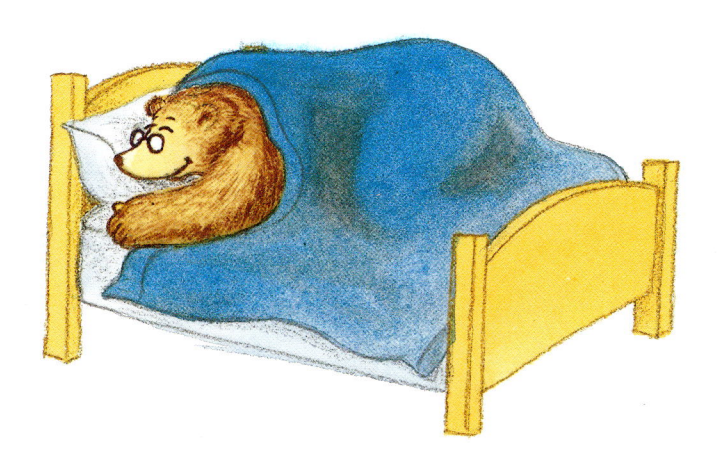

Here is Baby Bear.

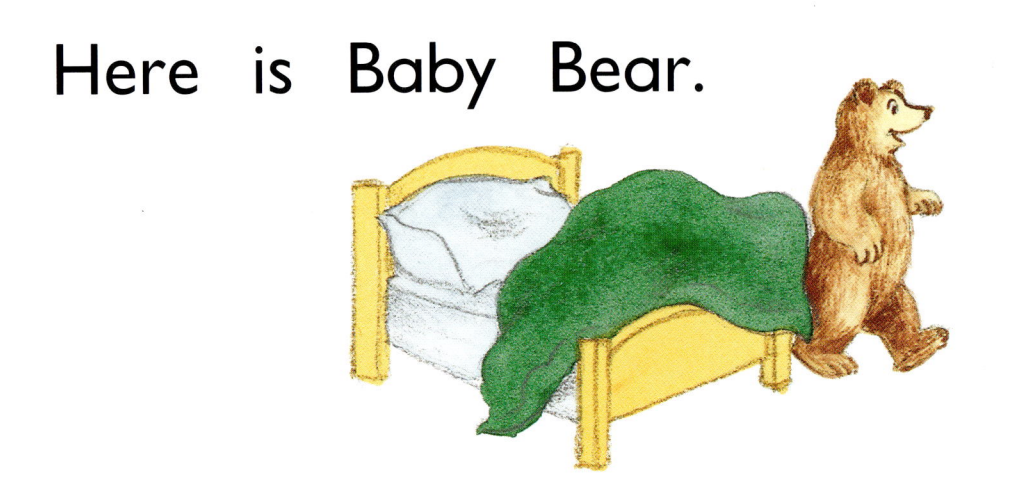

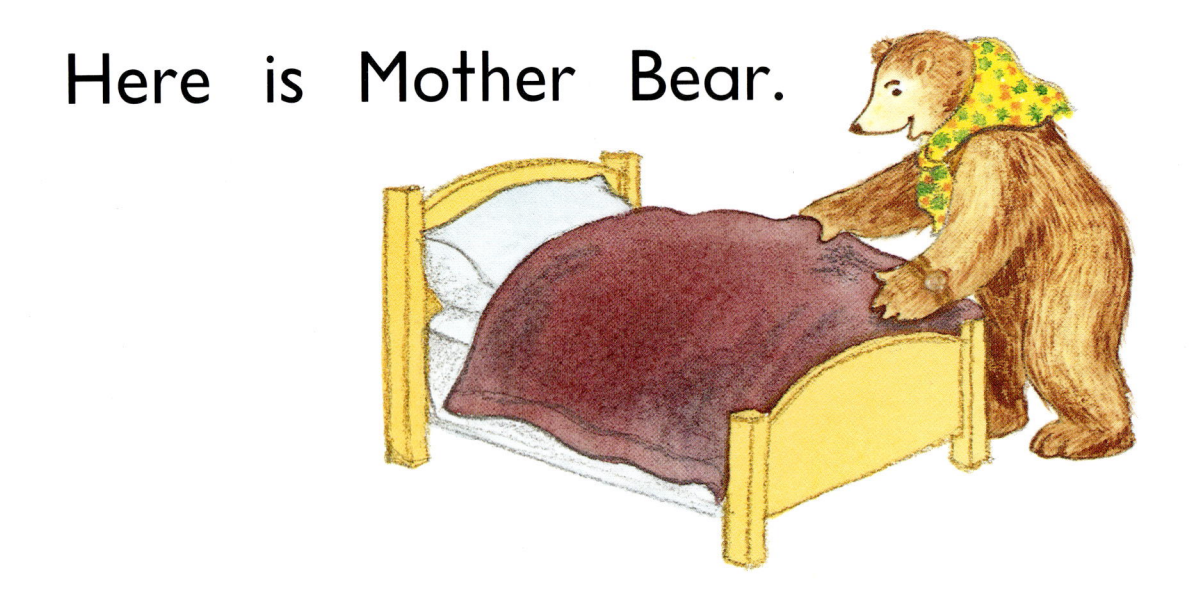

Here is Mother Bear.

Here is Father Bear.

Baby Bear is up.

Mother Bear is up.

5

Father Bear is in bed.

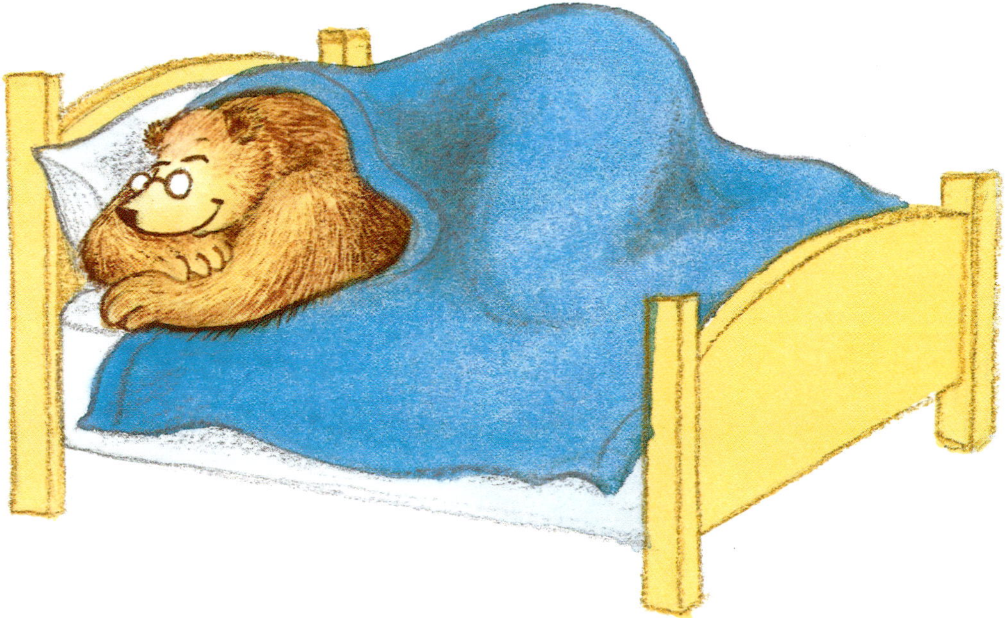

Baby Bear said,

"Wake up, Father Bear."

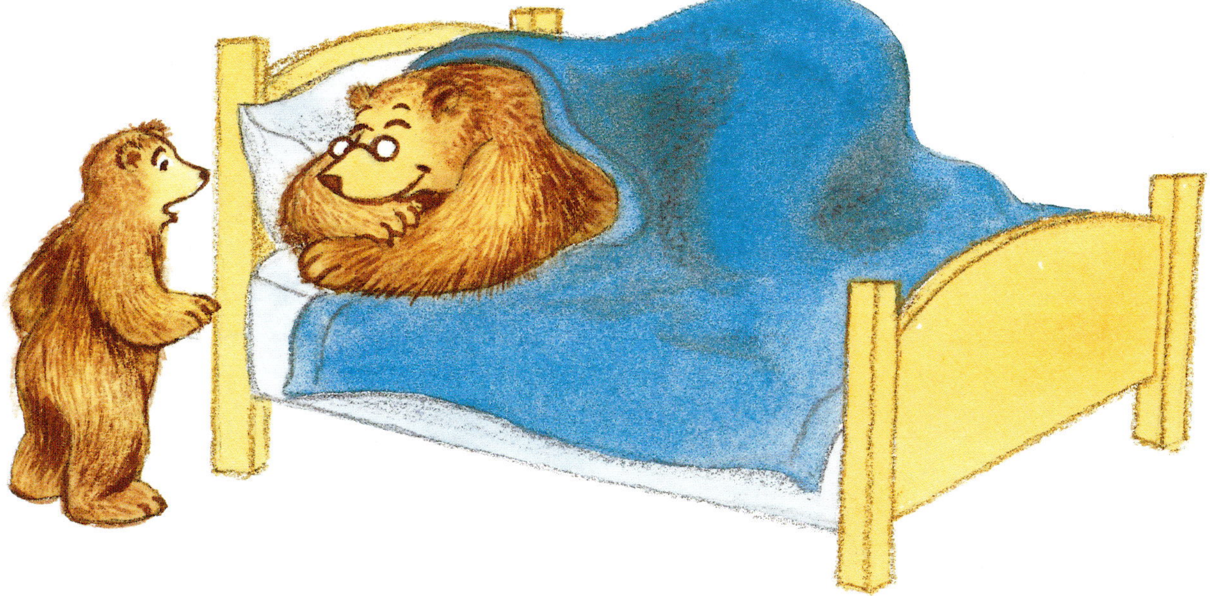

Mother Bear said,

"Wake up, Father Bear."

11

"Look at Father Bear,"

said Mother Bear.

"Look at Father Bear,"

said Baby Bear.

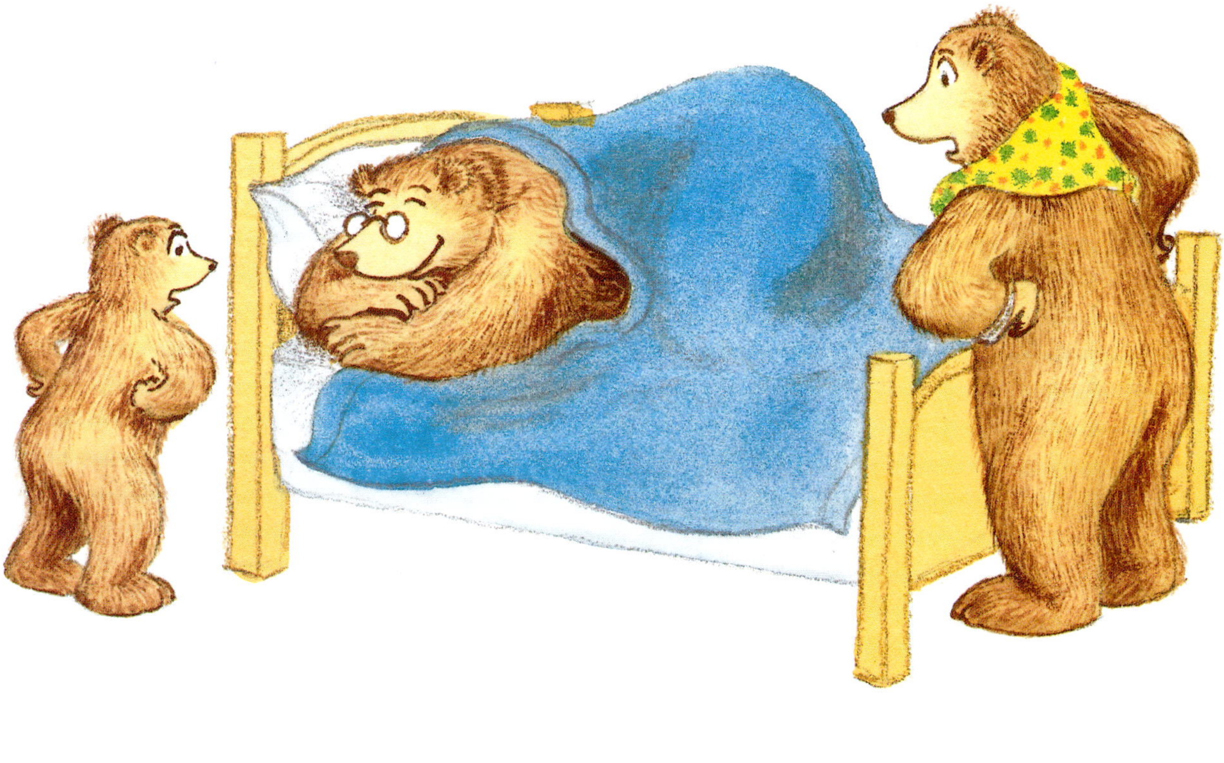

"Here I come!" said Baby Bear.

"Wake up, Father Bear."

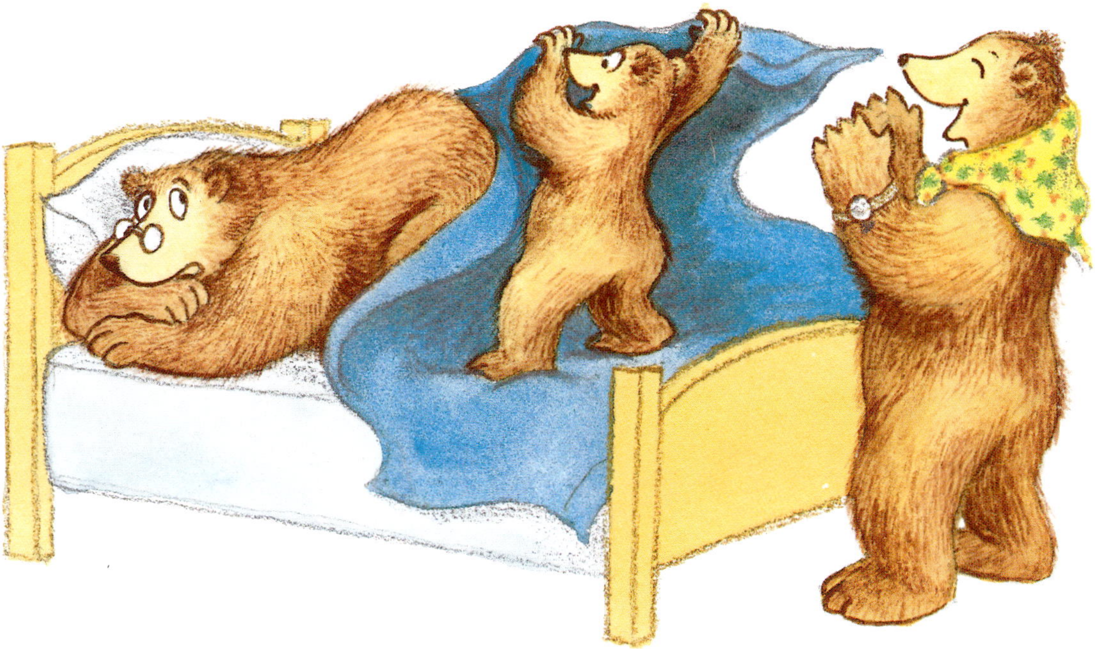

"I am up," said Father Bear.